"*Alex and the Scary Things* explains simple and effective coping strategies such as the 5-4-3-2-1 game in a playful and approachable way. This book can jumpstart conversations both with children who have experienced 'scary things' and with any child who is trying to make sense of challenging emotions."

—*Carlene MacMillan, MD, Adult and Child Psychiatrist, Trauma and Dissociative Unit, McLean Hospital, Harvard Medical School*

"This book is an excellent resource for parents, teachers, counselors, and anyone who works with children. Alex's story is endearing, tender, and relatable. Alex's kindness to himself and his parts will promote compassion and empathy in children—both for themselves and others. The exercises in the book will help readers participate with Alex while learning important skills to use for their own growth."

—*Nadja Reilly, Clinical Psychologist, Associate Director of the Freedman Center for Child and Family Development at the Massachusetts School of Professional Psychology*

of related interest

How Are You Feeling Today Baby Bear?
Exploring Big Feelings After Living in a Stormy Home
Jane Evans
Illustrated by Laurence Jackson
ISBN 978 1 84905 424 9
eISBN 978 0 85700 793 3

Using Stories to Build Bridges with Traumatized Children
Creative Ideas for Therapy, Life Story Work, Direct Work and Parenting
Kim S. Golding
Foreword by Steve Killick
ISBN 978 1 84905 540 6
eISBN 978 0 85700 961 6

Direct Work with Vulnerable Children
Playful Activities and Strategies for Communication
Audrey Tait and Helen Wosu
Foreword by Brigid Daniel
ISBN 978 1 84905 319 8
eISBN 978 0 85700 661 5

Melissa Moses

Illustrated by
Alison MacEachern

Alex
and the
Scary
Things

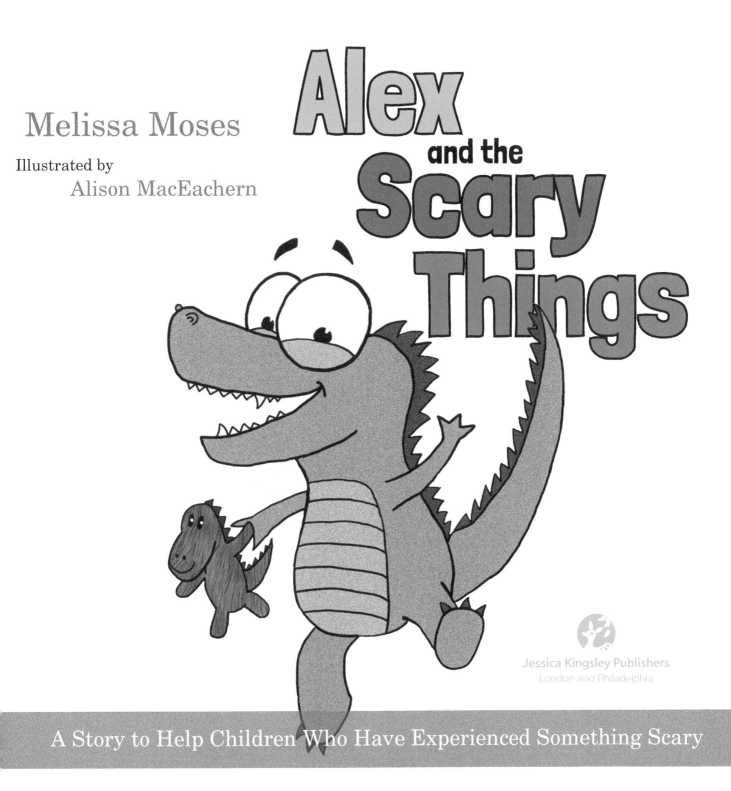

Jessica Kingsley Publishers
London and Philadelphia

A Story to Help Children Who Have Experienced Something Scary

First published in hardback in Great Britain in 2015
This paperback edition published in 2024 by Jessica Kingsley Publishers
An imprint of John Murray Press

1

A CIP catalogue record for this title is available from the British Library
and the Library of Congress

ISBN 978 1 80501 193 4
eISBN 978 1 78450 066 5

Printed and bound in Great Britain by Ashford Colour Press

Jessica Kingsley Publishers' policy is to use papers that are natural,
renewable and recyclable products and made from wood grown
in sustainable forests. The logging and manufacturing processes
are expected to conform to the environmental regulations
of the country of origin.

Jessica Kingsley Publishers
Carmelite House
50 Victoria Embankment
London EC4Y 0DZ

www.jkp.com

John Murray Press
Part of Hodder & Stoughton Ltd
An Hachette Company

For all the children who have experienced something scary
and need assistance handling those really big feelings.

Alison

And for Harper, who used to like asparagus.

Melissa

My name is Alex. I'm six years old.

I like to swing and dance and run and
make silly faces. My favorite food is
asparagus. I like to watch cartoons (when
I'm allowed) and I always win at bowling.

I also love doing science experiments.
Ms. Murphy, my teacher, lets me
get as messy as I want!

I have a stuffed Alligator.

His name is Al.

Al and I go on all kinds of adventures. We pretend to be pirates, we create massive LEGO® battles, and we like to play hide and seek. I always find Al. We're trying to learn how to become invisible, but Al isn't very good at it.

Al is the nicest stuffed Alligator ever
and he always tries to make me happy.
Usually it works. Sometimes it doesn't.

Some scary things have happened to me.
I try not to think about them.

When I remember those things, I feel my
heart beating really fast and I jump every
time I hear a loud noise. Sometimes I
shut my eyes super tight and I try really
hard to make the memories disappear.

I wish that someone could keep me safe.

I've learned that I have lots of parts in me. One part of me loves going to school and another part of me wants to stay outside and play all day.

Some parts of me
keep me safe when
I think about the scary things.

When I remember scary things,
I become Spacey.

When I'm Spacey, I go far away from the fear.

So far away that I disappear into the sky. I fly by clouds and stars and airplanes and spaceships and the moon. My space suit keeps me warm and safe and I'm not afraid of anything.

Sometimes when I'm Spacey I don't really know
where I go. I can be sitting watching cartoons
with Al and suddenly I become Spacey.

The next thing I know, the cartoon is over and I don't even know how it ended.

Sometimes I don't want to become Spacey. When I'm at school and I feel myself starting to fly away, I remember to play the 5-4-3-2-1 game. I name 5 things that I *see* in the room…the clock, the colorful flowers that we made to celebrate spring, the back of Malik's head, Ralphie the class robot, and the picture of all the letters in the alphabet. Then I name 4 things I can *feel*…my blue pencil, my chair, my toes wiggling in my sneakers, and the hard top of my desk.

Then I name 3 things I can *hear*…the clock ticking, markers marking, and Cindy and Jessica whispering. Then I name 2 things I can *smell*…the yummy smelling eraser that I keep in my desk and the lunches that are kept in the closet where we hang our coats. Last, I name 1 good thing about myself…I can run really fast. After I've done this, I don't have to be Spacey and I can listen to Ms. Murphy when she reads stories aloud. I love listening to stories.

Can you play the 5-4-3-2-1 game?

Sometimes the scary things make me feel
so mad that I become The Destroyer.

When I'm The Destroyer, I smash and slam and pound and crash into things and sometimes into other people. When I'm The Destroyer, not even Al can calm me down.

And then The Destroyer stops.

And I feel bad.

When I'm The Destroyer, my face turns
red and my muscles feel really tight.

When I stop, I like to lie down on the floor and
practice breathing like I'm smelling a flower—in
through my nose...and then blowing out candles...
whoosh—out through my mouth. In through my
nose...then whoosh—out through my mouth.

Can you practice breathing like you're smelling a flower, and then blowing out like you're trying to blow out all the candles on a birthday cake?

I'm not the only one in my class who can turn into The Destroyer.

Sometimes, after lunch, Ms. Murphy has the whole class do yoga to help us calm down. My favorite thing to do is Tree. Ms. Murphy tells us to stand on one leg and balance the other on the thigh of our standing leg. It's fun trying to balance and then Ms. Murphy asks us to raise our arms up and pretend they are branches swaying in the breeze.

Sometimes this makes us
lose our balance, but
we just try again.

Mainly we try not to
fall into other trees!

Sometimes I feel so sad. My arms and legs feel heavy and my heart hurts and I don't want to get out of bed or go to school or even play with Al. That's when I become Puddles

When I'm Puddles, I cry and cry.

Sometimes I know why. Sometimes I don't.

When I'm Puddles, I sit in my super-secret safe space where there are soft and snuggly blankets and lots of fluffy pillows that make me feel like I'm cuddling up in a cloud.

Al always comes to my super-secret safe space. He knows that Puddles needs to cry until there aren't any more tears. Then he starts making funny faces at me and tells me jokes, and I start to laugh and tell my own jokes and Puddles goes away.

Do you know any jokes?

Sometimes on the playground or in the classroom, other kids yell and run and everything seems too fast and it feels like scary things are happening even though they aren't. My tummy feels a little tumbly and my brain is a little bumbly.

When that happens, I become Jumbles. When I am Jumbles, I don't really know what is going on and I even get confused when I'm playing hide-and-seek.

And you know how good I am at hide-and-seek!

When I'm Jumbles, with a tumbly tummy and a bumbly brain, I remember to breathe like a volcano. I breathe in through my nose and bring my arms up...up...

and then I erupt like a volcano and all my breath comes out and my arms come down—BOOM!

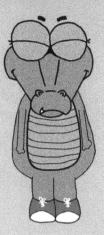

And then I squeeze my muscles together stiff and tight...tight...tight.

And then I let them go and I'm floppy like cooked spaghetti. When I'm all noodley, I like to do a wiggly dance. My friends like to dance with me. We laugh together and my tummy stops being tumbly and my brain isn't bumbly anymore.

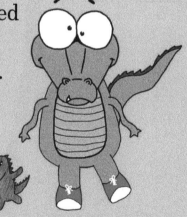

Can you do a floppy spaghetti wiggly dance?

Sometimes grown-ups ask me to talk about the
scary things. I don't always like talking. Sometimes
I don't even know what to say. I start to feel like
hiding or running away. Then I become Scribbles.

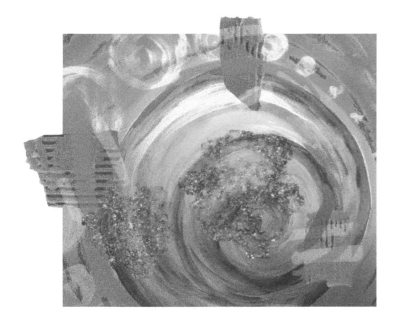

When I'm Scribbles, I paint all the colors swirling around. I add stickers and glitter and pipe cleaners and scotch tape and ribbon… Scribbles uses everything! Scribbles often leaves me with art projects that need to dry overnight.

And I usually feel better.

Most of the time, I am Alex. When I'm Alex, I feel calm and capable and curious and creative and kind. I finish all my work at school and I think of super fun games to play with my friends and I let Al win when we go bowling.

What are you like when you're you?

When I remember scary things, different parts of me keep me safe. Sometimes I need Spacey, The Destroyer, Puddles, Jumbles, and Scribbles. And sometimes I don't. I am learning to tell the difference. Well, most of the time. Other times, safe grown-ups help me understand different parts of me.

I love all of my parts and my parts love me. They help me when I need them and usually listen to me when I ask them to stay away. Scary things will always be scary. But Spacey, The Destroyer, Puddles, Jumbles, and Scribbles will try to keep me safe.

Do you have parts like Alex?

Note to Caregivers

Children who experience trauma express its impact in numerous ways. Children may have greater difficulty developing relationships with peers; they may struggle to regulate arousal, impulses, and behaviors; and they may experience the effects of dissociation (detachment from immediate surroundings or from physical and emotional experiences). Children may experience a continued sense of failure that can shape their sense of self.

To help children retain a sense of competency and self-worth, adults can help give them language to externalize behaviors that can be viewed as problematic. This allows children to understand that they are not the problem; rather, "parts" of themselves act in different ways. Some behaviors or parts are adaptive when surviving or coping with traumatic experiences. However, many of these same behaviors or parts may interfere with concentration, communication, and interactions with others. Grounded in theory from Internal Family Systems (IFS) therapy, the aim of this book is to give parents, teachers, and caregivers a language for these behaviors by naming them "parts." When behaviors or "parts" are expressed at inappropriate times, the child and caregiver can help identify and manage them without fear or shame.

When children experience scary things, it can be difficult for them to talk about the events or feelings directly. The intention of this book is to allow a child to understand what different parts do without having to reflect on the reasons they emerged. The storyline acknowledges a variety of parts and offers coping strategies in a playful way. Practicing the breathing techniques and the relaxation activities with children will help them learn self-regulation skills to help them manage intense emotions or experiences. It is recommended that readers engage children in a discussion about their own parts—do they have a part like Spacey? Does that part have a name? This will help personalize the ideas presented in the story of Alex and his parts. Additionally, children can draw pictures of their parts or find stuffed animals that represent them. As readers, you can help children think about when they need the different parts, and how to heal the different parts. If they are uncomfortable talking about their parts right away, there is no need to press the issue. However, it may be helpful to readdress the idea of parts by externalizing behaviors that are playful, for example "It looks like you've become your Candy Monster part!" when a child wants more and more sweets.

Though this book is written from a trauma-informed perspective, it is intended for everyone. Breathing techniques, mood monitoring, and grounding strategies can be useful for all children and adults. In fact, children benefit from seeing the grown-ups in their lives model coping skills! We hope you enjoy the story and we thank you for caring for children.